CROSS STITCH

CROSS STITCH

HILARY MORE

SERIES EDITOR: ROSEMARY WILKINSON

CHARTWELL
BOOKS, INC.

Note: Imperial and metric measurements are not direct equivalents, so always follow only one set in a particular method.

Published by
CHARTWELL BOOKS, INC.
A Division of BOOK SALES, INC.
110 Enterprise Avenue
Secaucus, New Jersey 07094

Created and produced by
Rosemary Wilkinson and Malcolm Saunders Publishing Ltd
4 Lonsdale Square, London N1 1EN

ISBN 0-7858-0008-5

Produced by Mandarin Offset
Printed and bound in
Hong Kong

Illustrations: Terry Evans
Design: Ming Cheung
Cover photograph: by courtesy of DMC, 10, Avenue Ledru-Rollin,
F-75579 Paris, Cedex 12, France

Contents

Introduction

Counted cross stitch, also known as sampler stitch, is one of the oldest and most widely used embroidery stitches. Cross stitch is composed of two diagonal stitches worked one on top of the other over an evenweave fabric or canvas. Counted stitches need no tracings or transfers as each stitch is worked over an exact number of threads. All around the world different versions of this stitch can be found in traditional embroideries.

Records of the different patterns were stitched in the form of samplers and kept as a personal collection of favourite patterns. These samplers are highly prized as collectors' items today.

Cross stitch can also be worked on uneven and pile fabrics by stitching over a grid of canvas tacked to the fabric, which is then removed. Also, some modern embroiderers work free cross stitch using a variety of threads over any type of fabric. These stitches are, therefore, not controlled by the fabric weave and vary in size and direction.

Part 1:
EQUIPMENT

Fabric

Although cross stitch can be worked on many different types of materials, using the fabric threads as a guide is the easiest way of placing the stitches accurately and creating the designs. An evenweave fabric, which has the same number of weft (horizontal) and warp (vertical) threads in any square inch (centimetre) will help to produce the perfect cross stitch.

Evenweave linens and cottons are the most common fabrics for cross stitch. Use cotton for items, such as clothes, cushion covers and mats that need to be hardwearing and washable, and linen for table and bed linen. Both these fabrics are available in a variety of thread counts, that is the number of threads to the inch (2.5cm). The coarsest fabric has 6 to 8 threads per inch (2.5cm) while the fine fabrics have 30 to 36 threads per inch (2.5cm). The higher the number, the finer the fabric and stitch. Cross stitches are usually worked over two threads of fabric.

Evenweave fabrics only come in a narrow range of colours, so search through the dress and furnishing fabrics for other evenweave fabrics which could also be used.

Aida fabric

This is the most popular of the evenweave fabrics. It is available in thread counts of 7, 8, 10, 11, 14 and 18 and in a variety of colours, with white and ecru being the most common. Aida is also produced in bands for decorative edging strips or bookmarks, as well as in the usual fabric widths.

Binca fabric
This evenweave fabric is similar to Aida but is woven with 6 blocks to 1in (2.5cm) and is often used by children working their first piece of embroidery.

Fancy weaves
There is also a variety of fancy weaves which incorporate evenweave areas, specially designed to take cross stitch embroidery, e.g. damask fabrics with squares suitable for embroidered table linen and guest towels and babies' bibs with a band ready for a cross stitch design.

Hardanger fabric
This evenweave fabric is woven with double threads intersecting, while Aida and Binca are woven in blocks of threads.

Threads
Embroidery threads come in different types and colours and the rule is to use a thread similar in thickness to the fabric so it will cover up the background.

Before beginning any project it is a good idea to work a sample first with your chosen fabric and thread, to gauge the covering and size of stitch.

Stranded cotton
This is the most versatile embroidery thread. It is made up of six loosely twisted strands which can be used as a single thread or in any multiple, ideal for cross stitch as the varied thread amounts can bring

depth and contrast to a design. Stranded cotton comes in a wide range of colours.

Stranded silk
A thread made up of four loosely twisted strands, which can be divided as required. The silk gives a luxurious sheen to the embroidery and is available in a limited range of colours.

Perlé or pearl cotton
A shiny twisted single 2-ply thread which comes in three thickness from 3, 5 and 8 (3 is the thickest and 5 is the most commonly available). Perlé (pearl) cotton comes in a good colour range including some shaded colours.

Coton à broder
This is a fine, flat cotton thread with a slight sheen. This thread cannot be separated.

Soft embroidery cotton
A tightly twisted 5-ply matt cotton thread. This thread cannot be separated.

Danish flower thread
This is a fine matt cotton which comes in a single strand ready to stitch.

Viscose embroidery thread
A high lustre four-stranded thread that can be split for stitching.

Metallic threads
These threads are now very popular, particularly as the range of colours and thicknesses increases.

They come in gold, silver and many other sparkling shades.

Tapestry wool
A lightly twisted 4-ply wool which comes in a good range of colours.

Crewel wool
A fine 2-ply wool.

Persian wool
A loosely twisted 3-ply wool.

Also look among the knitting and handsewing threads for different yarns and threads that can be used over embroidery fabrics. If you are in any doubt, work a small sample with your chosen thread and fabric to see the result before embarking on a large project and adjust the materials accordingly.

Thread organizer

When working with a variety of different coloured threads it is a good idea to store them on an organiser. These can quickly be made from a sheet of stiff card.

Cut a strip of card and punch holes vertically down one long side. Thread each differently coloured skein through one of the holes, then write the number of the thread alongside. In this way the threads will not get muddled up in the workbox. This is also a useful way of keeping a record of the threads used in a particular project.

Ready-punched cards and record sheets are commercially available.

Needles

Blunt-ended **tapestry needles** with large eyes should be used for cross stitch since they will not split the threads as they pass through the fabric. They come in a range of sizes from 13 to 26.

When working on fine fabric you will need to use **crewel needles** which have sharp points. They are available in sizes 1-10.

Remember, the higher the number, the shorter and finer the needle. The needle eye must be large enough to accommodate the thread smoothly, if it is a tight fit, the thread will fray easily. To gauge the best size for your chosen fabric, make sure that the threaded needle is able to pass through the fabric without pushing the threads apart.

The following table gives details of which needle to use with which thread count of fabric, alongside suggestions for suitable projects for the different fabric sizes.

THREAD COUNT	THREADS & THICKNESS	NEEDLE SIZE	PROJECTS
8 + 11	perlé cotton 3	22	beginners'
14	perlé cotton 5 stranded cotton or silk – 3 strands	24	bookmarks, cards
16	stranded cotton or silk – 2 strands	26	samplers
18	stranded cotton or silk – 2 strands single flower threads	26	samplers, cards, pictures
22	stranded cotton or silk – 2 strands	26	samplers, pictures
25	stranded cotton or silk – 1 strand	26	bell pulls, pictures
28	stranded cotton or silk – 1 strand	26	cushions
32	stranded cotton or silk– 1 strand	26	very fine detailed work, flower pictures

Hoops

While not totally necessary for Aida and Binca
fabrics, an embroidery hoop is a must for most
evenweave fabrics. It will hold the fabric taut while
you stitch, making it easier to work the stitches.

Composed of two wooden rings that fit snugly one
inside the other, the outer ring has an adjustable
screw, to allow the hoop to cope with different
thickness of fabric. Embroidery hoops range in size
from 4in (10cm) upwards and can also be fixed to
adjustable stands, which leave both hands free for
stitching the embroidery.

Scissors

Use a large pair of dressmaking scissors for cutting
out the fabric pieces. When stitching, use a small
pair of embroidery scissors, approximately 5in
(12.5cm) long with pointed tips. Avoid using these
scissors for any other work as you will blunt the
ends and the blades.

Masking tape

This is used on the edges of the fabric to protect
your hands and clothes while stitching and also to
prevent the fabric from fraying.

Other useful equipment

Tape measure for measuring accurately.

Needle threader if you find threading needles a
problem.

A **daylight bulb** fitted into your reading/sewing lamp is a must when embroidering during the evening, it will provide a good light which is essential when counting threads of fabric and choosing thread colours.

A **magnifying glass** can be a useful aid when working from a chart. Various types are available, such as a line magnifier, which will magnify a chart line by line or an illuminated glass for use in poor light conditions. Some glasses are supplied with cords, so that they can be hung round your neck leaving your hands free to stitch.

For drawing up your own charts you will need **ruler**, **pens** and **crayons**, **traced grid paper**, or **graph paper** and **plain tracing paper**.

Part 2:
TECHNIQUES

CUTTING AND BINDING THE FABRIC

Cut a piece of fabric at least 3in (7.5cm) larger all around than the finished design.

To cut the embroidery fabric to size, trim along a thread line or pull out a single thread from across the fabric and cut along the gap.

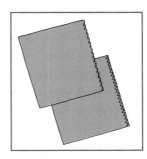

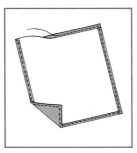

To prevent the fabric from fraying, either bind the edges with masking tape by folding it evenly in half over the raw edges or overcast the edges by hand with a contrasting thread. The edges can also be finished on a sewing machine either with a zigzag stitch or by straight stitching a narrow hem.

MARKING OUT THE FABRIC

Cross stitch designs are usually worked from a chart
so it will be easier to position the stitches centrally
on the fabric if the fabric is divided into quarters to
match the dividing arrows on the chart. On a small
piece of evenweave fabric you can count the
threads along each edge of the fabric to find the
centre point. Alternatively, fold the fabric in half
both horizontally and vertically. On a large piece it
will be simplest to find the centre vertical and
horizontal lines by measuring.

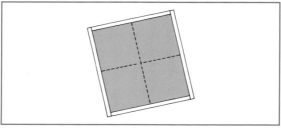

Using a tacking thread in a contrasting colour and
tapestry needle, join up the marks across the fabric
horizontally and vertically with tacking stitches.
These tacked lines should correspond with marked
centre lines on the chart.

WORKING FROM A CHART

Cross stitch charts are divided into a grid of squares
with each square representing one cross stitch. The
cross stitch is worked over a block of threads, i.e. an
intersection of warp and weft threads.

A solid continuous black line on a chart will
indicate a line of back stitching or Holbein stitch,

which can outline or highlight part of a cross stitch design.

The centre horizontal and vertical lines of the chart are marked by arrows and these must match up with the tacked lines on the fabric. If the centre of the chart is not marked, count across the edges in the same way as for the fabric and mark the centre lines with arrows.

The starting point for stitching the design may also be marked.

The charts will be either in colour or in black and white with different symbols denoting the different shades.

PREPARING THE THREADS

Cut the working thread no longer than 16in (40cm). Find the thread end in the skein of embroidery thread and holding the skein band, gentle pull out the required length.

Stranded cotton should always be separated into six

strands and then the required number of strands rejoined ready for stitching. To separate the strands, hold the cut lengths and gently pull out each strand.

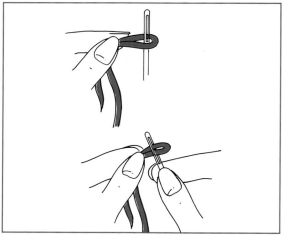

To thread the needle, wrap the thread(s) over the needle eye and hold tight. Slip the thread loop off the needle and push the loop through the eye.

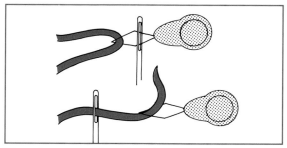

If you have a problem threading needles use a needle threader. Push the needle threader through the eye of the needle. Loop the thread through the

threader and pull it back though the needle eye
complete with thread.

USING AN EMBROIDERY HOOP

Never leave a piece of work stored in an
embroidery hoop, as heavy crease marks will be left
in the fabric.

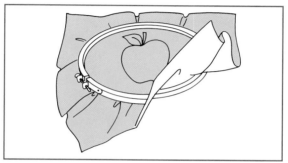

1 Separate the two rings by loosening the screw of
the larger ring. With the right side uppermost, place
the fabric centrally over the smaller ring. Place the
larger outer ring over the fabric.

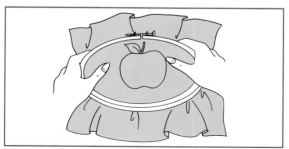

2 Gently press down evenly all around. Adjust the
screw until the fabric is taut.

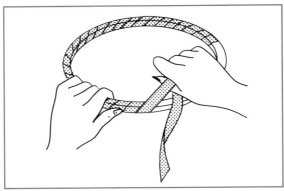

3 To prevent the rings from damaging the fabric, bind around the smaller inner ring with cotton tape or masking tape. Hold the end of the tape firmly and wind around and around the ring covering the tape end. At the other end, tuck under the end and fasten with a few oversewn stitches.

4 When working a large embroidery, try to position the whole of a motif in the centre of the ring.

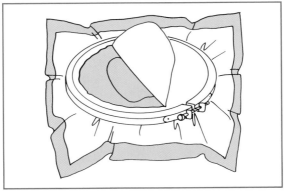

After moving the hoop to a new position, cover the

worked sections with tissue paper to protect them. It is simplest to cover the whole area of the hoop with tissue paper, then tear away the paper covering the unworked areas.

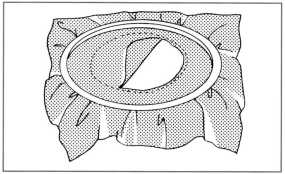

5 If the fabric is smaller than the embroidery hoop, hand stitch the embroidery fabric to a scrap of backing fabric that is large enough to fit in the hoop. Fit the backing fabric into the hoop in the usual way, then cut away the backing fabric behind the area to be embroidered.

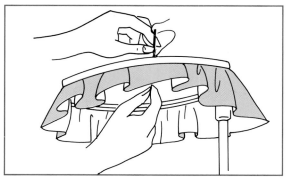

6 If you are working with your hoop on a fixed

stand, you can use both hands to work the stitches, one on top and the other beneath the fabric.

Tangled threads

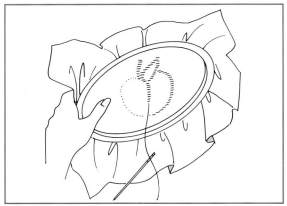

To untangle a working thread, let go of the needle and let the thread hang vertically. When it stops twisting, the thread will have straightened itself.

BEGINNING TO STITCH

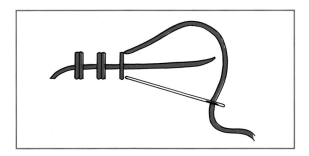

When you begin, bring the needle through the fabric to the right side, leaving a short tail of thread on the wrong side. Hold this thread against the back of the fabric and work with first few cross stitches over this end to hold the thread firmly in the fabric. Alternatively leave the end hanging free and darn it into the back of the work when the embroidery is complete.

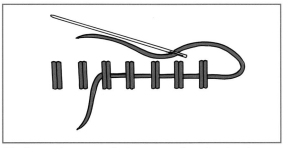

To fasten the start of subsequent threads, simply slide the needle under a few worked stitches on the wrong side of the fabric and bring the needle to the front of the work.

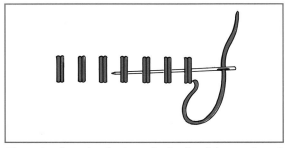

To end a thread, take it to the back of the work and darn it through the back of a few stitches. Trim off against the fabric.

WORKING CROSS STITCH ON PATTERNED FABRICS

Some fabrics have a natural grid-like weave and cross stitch can be worked over this without too much trouble. Gingham and similar checked fabric are good examples. Gingham comes with different check sizes and if you place a cross in each square this will determine the size of the stitches. The woven squares are either white or coloured, so by placing the cross stitches on either the white or the coloured squares or a combination of the two, further design alternatives become available, as shown in the diagram opposite.

Try working with a coloured thread and stitching the crosses on the coloured squares to underline the contrast between the coloured and white squares or work the crosses in the white squares to give the fabric a more even appearance.

1 Bring the needle out of the fabric at the bottom righthand corner of the first square and take a diagonal stitch to the opposite corner of the square.

2 Bring the needle out again vertically below in the left-hand corner and take another diagonal stitch across the square into the fabric at the top right-hand corner.

3 Either miss out the next square of gingham or continue working a cross in each square.

WITHDRAWN OR WASTE CANVAS
Use this method to work an even cross stitch design over an uneven fabric, a fabric with a pile, such as

velvet, or over an evenweave fabric whose threads are too fine to count.

1 Mark out the chosen area on the fabric. You will need a piece of fine single thread (not interlocked) canvas of the correct gauge (threads per inch/2.5cm) for the motif, cut to the same size as the area plus a little extra all around. Using a contrasting thread, tack the canvas through the centre both ways to anchor it to the fabric. Check that the canvas threads match the grainlines of the fabric both horizontally and vertically, then tack around the outer edge.

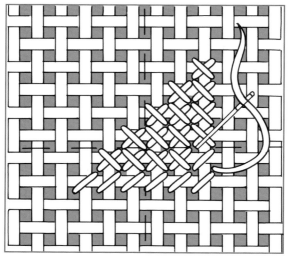

2 Following the chart, work the cross stitches over the canvas and through the fabric. Make sure that you take the needle straight down through the canvas and through the fabric. Check the tension of the stitches, they should be firm but not too tight.

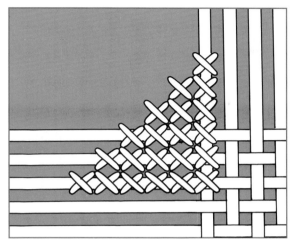

3 When the embroidery is complete, carefully remove the tacking stitches, then snip and remove the canvas threads one by one with tweezers, from top to bottom and then from side to side.

RANDOM STITCHING

When working free-style cross stitch, the stitches do not have to be worked over a counted fabric so a variety of different fabrics can be used. To gain more unusual effects layer fabrics together combining cut shapes and different fabrics – sheers and wools or even velvet – can be used as a background to cross stitch.

Clever stitchery can be combined with patterned fabrics, for example, try working a design on a striped fabric using the stripes as part of the design and working the crosses in the light strips in between the dark ones.

Fabric woven with deep ridges or bands can be cross stitched in the same way. In some diagonal weaves the crosses can be set in the troughs of the fabric.

Damask is another perfect fabric for stitching. The design has been already woven into the fabric so random cross stitching can be worked to outline the shapes or to fill in certain areas. Experiment with fabrics in your scrap bag to explore a different range of results.

PAINTING FABRIC BEFORE STITCHING

Fabric dyes and paints have opened a new world to embroiderers over the years. Plain white fabric can often look too boring for the design you have in mind, but by giving it a colour wash before you begin to stitch, the result is suddenly enhanced.

The fabric need not be painted in solid outlines, colours can be merged together or allowed to bleed across the fabric producing a more natural effect.

You can combine fabric painting with cross stitch, so that some areas are left with the painted design, while in others detail and texture are added through cross stitching.

Fabric paints

A good variety of paints is sold alongside fabric and threads in haberdashery departments and craft shops. The paint can be applied to the fabric with a brush or a sponge, it can be sprayed over the fabric or air-brushed for a diffused effect.

Always practise on a spare piece of fabric before you begin the actual design.

1 Before using a fabric paint, wash and dry the fabric to remove any finish which will prevent the paint from being absorbed by the fabric.

2 Only a small amount of dye will be needed to cover a small area of fabric, so pour a little into a saucer. Test the paint on a sample of fabric and then if the colour is too strong dilute it gradually with teaspoons of water until the chosen shade is reached.

3 Paint a few samples and leave to dry to check the results. Fabric paint colours can also be mixed together, the options are endless.

DESIGNING CROSS STITCH CHARTS

Designing your own chart will produce a unique piece of embroidery. As cross stitch is worked in evenly formed blocks designing a chart is not hard to do with the use of tracing and graph paper. Also available is traced grid paper which is tracing paper ready printed with a grid.

Choose a motif or design with a clear outline but remember that as you draw up the design you can always leave out various sections or simplify any complicated edges.

A well-spaced background is essential to a good
design. You may need to redraw the design several
times until the result looks ready for stitching.
If you are worried about your ability to draw
objects or motifs, trace off a design from a book, a
magazine or from one of the printed labels from
bottles or packages around the house – just look
about for suitable motifs.

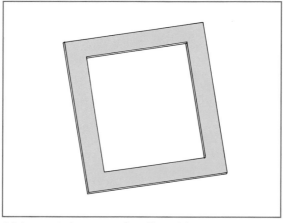

Make a window out of cardboard by cutting a
square of card; mark and cut out the centre. Use
this when searching for suitable motifs as it will help
to isolate the motifs and give you an impression of
what a chosen shape will look like by itself.

1 Pick out your motif or design and tape it flat on a
surface. Cut a piece of tracing or traced graph paper
and tape it flat over the design. Using a sharp pencil
or fine-tipped marking pen, draw around the outline of the design. (Follow the outline of the squares
if using traced graph paper.) Alter the outline as

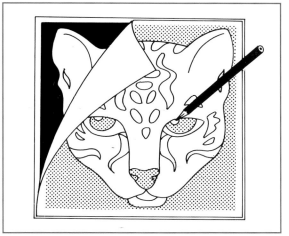

necessary to gain a more even motif. Add in the details within the outline.

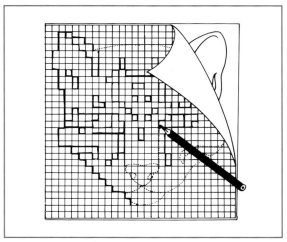

2 Cut a piece of graph paper to the same size as the tracing paper. Transfer the outline from the tracing paper to the graph paper. Match the grids together if using traced graph paper.

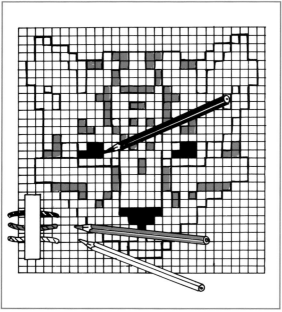

3 Use crayons or coloured felt tip pens to colour in the outline. Either follow the original colours of the motif or change the shades to suit your idea. To try out different colourways, photostat the design and colour it in different colours until you have the result you want. To help match the crayon colours to thread colours make a key at the side of the drawing, colour in a square of graph paper and tape a short length of the chosen thread beside it.

4 To soften the outline, add half squares around certain sections of the design, these can be worked

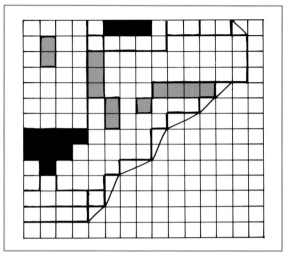

in back stitch when the motif is embroidered.

5 Choose the fabric on which to embroider the motif. This will determine the finished size and thread you need to cover the fabric. Count up the horizontal squares on the charted design, then count the vertical squares.

For example, when a motif covering 40 x 30 squares is worked using a fabric with 10 threads to 1in (2.5cm) the finished motif will measure 4 x 3in (10 by 7.5cm). By using a fabric with 8 threads to 1in (2.5cm) the motif size will increase to 5 x 3 ¾in (12.5 x 10cm). By working with a finer fabric with 20 threads to 1in (2.5cm) the motif will be a much smaller 2 x 1 ½in (5 x 4cm).

The design can also be distorted as you stitch it. To elongate a motif, work over two threads widthwise

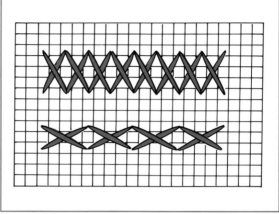

and over four threads when stitching lengthwise. You can shorten a motif by reversing this action. Experiment by working several samples of the same motif using different fabrics and threads.

DESIGNING A SAMPLER

Traditional samplers had a practical use – each one recorded a needlewoman's stitch and pattern library before charts and graph paper were available. Nowadays samplers are more often used to record a family event, such as a birth, wedding or special anniversary.

Generally a sampler is made up of a border pattern which is repeated on all four sides, with an alphabet and/or numbers and other motifs spaced over the fabric inside the border frame.

Both borders and motifs can be abstract or have a theme. A selection is given on pages 38 to 39.

Choose a neutral shade for the background fabric, so the message will stand out against large areas which remain unworked and exposed.

Borders

When designing a border, work from the centre out to each side. When the length is longer than the width the pattern will have to be adjusted to fit. And the corners will need special care (see page 44).

Centre design

Each section of the sampler can be designed separately, then reassembled on a larger sheet of graph paper.

Check that the eye is lead across the sampler or up and down and keep the horizontal and vertical lines to a minimum to prevent the design from looking too muddled.

Photocopy your design several times and use crayons or felt tip pens to colour in the sampler design with various colour options before you make your final choice.

The embroidered section can be worked either in muted old-fashioned shades to make it look like a traditional sampler or up-to-the-minute colours can be substituted for a modern interpretation.

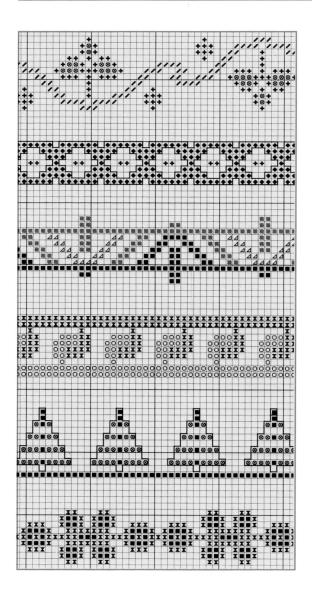

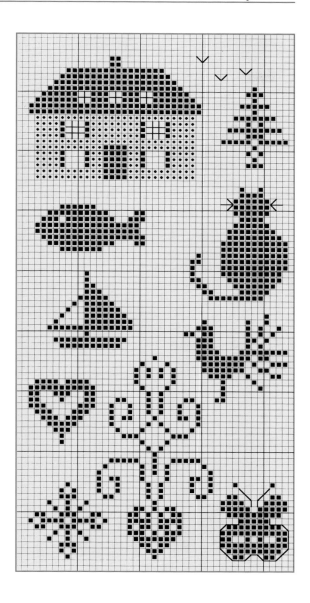

Letters and numbers

They are many different styles that can be used for the alphabet and numbers, just two examples are given below and on pages 41 to 43. If the sampler contains a message, the lettering must be easy to read, so choose a plain style, but if it is just composed of various letters and numbers, the style can be more elaborate.

First decide on the finished size then, as with motif designs, use graph paper to work out the letters.

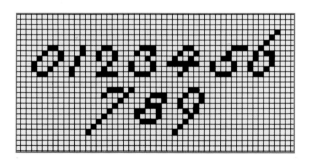

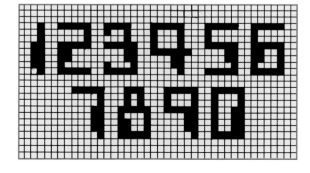

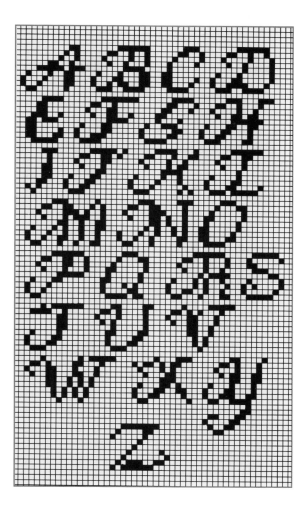

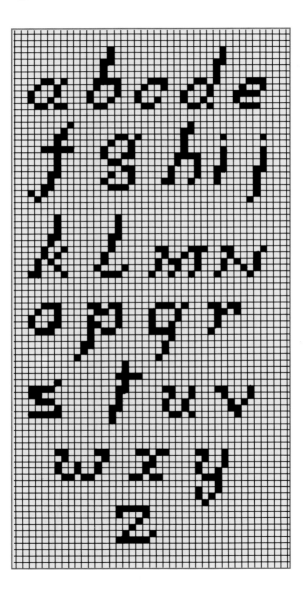

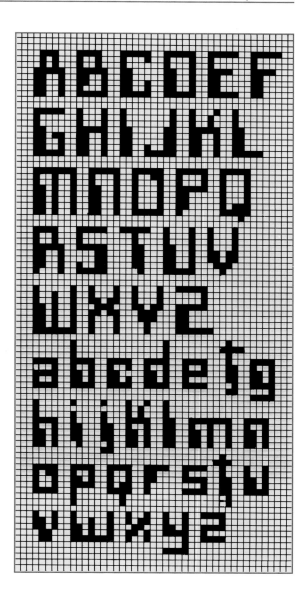

Creating a neat corner design

Use a mirror to create a good corner when designing a border or pattern.

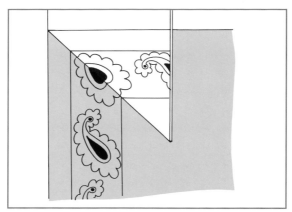

1 Place a small mirror diagonally across the design. Check the reflected image and move the mirror slowly down the border until the design looks good in the mirror.

2 Mark a line diagonally across the design, then remove the mirror.

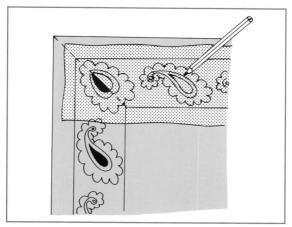

3 Cut and tape a piece of tracing paper over the design and trace off the design up to the diagonal line. Turn the tracing paper over and mark the design in reverse from the other side of diagonal line. Repeat at each corner of the design.

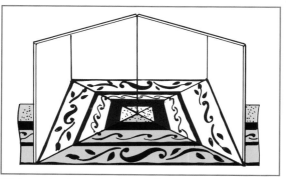

This method can also be used to create a square

design from a border design. Lay the border design horizontally on a flat surface. Place two mirrors at right angles to each other. Move the mirrors backwards and forwards until an attractive design is achieved, then mark both ends with diagonal lines and trace as before.

BLOCKING AND STRETCHING THE FINISHED EMBROIDERY

Not all cross stitch embroideries need blocking after they are finished. When the finished piece is to be framed as a picture stretching and pulling over a backing board might be all that is needed to bring the fabric back into shape. However, if you have worked the piece in the hand without a frame or if you feel that the fabric has been distorted, stretching it back into shape is a must.

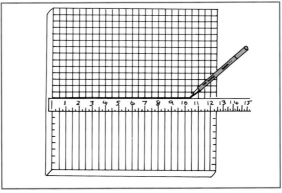

1 Mark out a board with a grid so the finished work can be lined up to a straight edge. Use an indelible marking pen, that will not mark the fabric when wet.

2 Provided the fabric and threads are colourfast and can be washed, soak the embroidery in cold water. Lay the piece right side up on a clean board. Place a drawing pin in each corner.

3 Gently pull out the sides to the correct size and

add more drawing pins evenly-spaced down each side and across the top and bottom.

4 If the fabric cannot be washed, just gently dampen around the outside edges of the work with a wet sponge and pull into shape.

MOUNTING CROSS STITCH IN A FRAME

Purchased frames have a backing board, glass and frame. If you are taking your embroidery to a picture framer, you may prefer to mount the fabric on a piece of backing board yourself. The picture framer will cut the board for you. It should be cut to fit the chosen frame size.

1 Remove the backing board from the frame. Lay the embroidery right side up centrally over the backing board. Stick pins into the edge of the board along the top edge.

2 Stretch the fabric over the bottom edge and add pins into the edges of the board. Check that the motif or picture remains centrally placed.

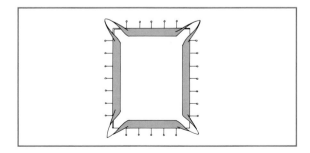

3 Repeat, pinning the fabric at both sides. Check that the motif is still central, adjust if necessary, then turn the board over.

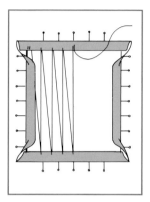
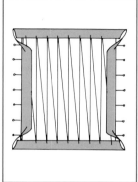

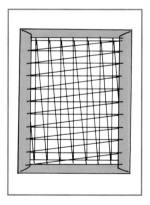

4 Using strong thread and working from the centre out to each edge in turn, lace the fabric edges together from top to bottom; fasten off. Then lace the side edges together across the back of the board and fasten off.

5 Turn the picture over, check the fabric is flat and the motif centrally placed and fit inside the frame.

To give the embroidery a softer surface, you can add a piece of thin wadding the same size as the backing board between the board and the fabric.

FITTING A DESIGN INTO A CARD MOUNT

Greetings cards are a popular and highly individualized way of displaying cross stitch designs. Card blanks are available commercially in a variety of shapes and sizes, but it is also possible to make your own.

1 Decide on the finished size of the card – the piece of cross stitch will help to determine the size. On a sheet of card, mark the square or rectangle card size three times, with edges butting together.

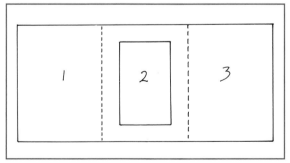

2 Place the card right side down on a work surface. In the centre piece, using a set square to obtain right angle sides, mark the window for the embroidery. Alternatively, use a pair of compasses to mark a circular centre section. Using a sharp craft knife against a ruler, carefully cut out the centre section and discard.

3 Using the back of a pair of scissors or a blunt tapestry needle, score along the marked edges of each card section.

4 Trim down the finished embroidery so that it is slightly smaller than the width of the central card section. If the fabric is likely to fray easily, overcast the edges by hand or zigzag stitch them on a sewing-machine.

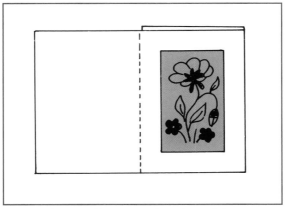

5 Spread clear adhesive on the edges of the upper-most face of the righthand side section. Press the embroidery, right side up, centrally over this section. Spread a little adhesive around the upper-most face of the window section, then fold over the righthand side, so that it lies on top, thereby sealing the embroidery inside the two sections. Tuck under the lefthand side to form the card.

FITTING A DESIGN TO SCROLL ENDS

Bell-pulls and banners can best be displayed by attaching scroll ends at the top and bottom of the embroidered piece. These decorative ends can be purchased from needlework suppliers and will incorporate a hanging device.

To fit these scroll ends onto the embroidery, work as follows:

1 Decide on the finished length – the size of the ends will determine the width – and embroider the fabric allowing 1in (2.5cm) on the side edges and 2in (5cm) at top and base for hems.

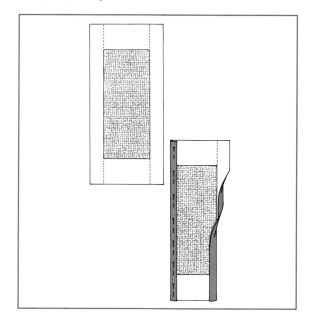

2 Cut a piece of iron-on interfacing to the finished size of the bell pull and fuse centrally to the wrong side of a piece of lining; trim the lining to match the interfacing edges.

3 Place the interfaced lining centrally to the wrong side of the embroidered fabric. Turn over the side edges of the fabric and fold under the raw edge to form a neat hem, then slipstitch in place to the lining.

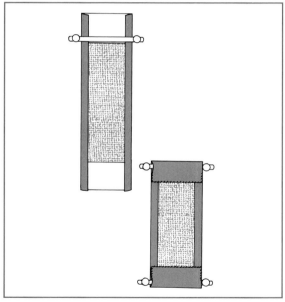

4 Slide the top scroll section over the raw edges of the embroidery fabric at the top. Turn under the raw edge, forming a neat hem and slipstitch to the back of the bell pull. Add the base scroll end in the same way.

Part 3:
STITCHES

CROSS STITCH

Cross stitch can be worked from right to left or from left to right as long as the upper stitches on all the crosses in the design lie in the same direction.

As with all embroidery and canvaswork, always try to come up into a empty hole and go down in a partially filled hole, to smooth down the thread.

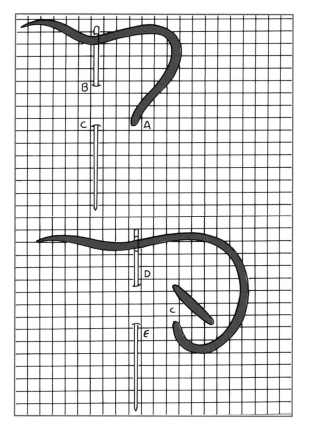

1 Bring the needle and thread through the fabric at A (see page 55). Take a diagonal stitch across the fabric and insert the needle through the fabric at B, three threads up and three threads to the left.

2 Bring the needle out again at C vertically below to complete the half cross stitch.

Cross stitch rows

3 When working a row of cross stitch, continue stitching half cross stitch across the fabric as shown, forming the next stitch by inserting the needle at D, three threads up and three threads to the left of C and bringing it out at E. In at F and out at G.

4 To complete the cross stitches, work the same stitches back over the half cross stitches, in the opposite direction (see page 57). Come out of the fabric at G and insert at D. Continue in this way to the end of the row.

Single cross stitch

5 If working a single cross stitch, work from A to B as in the first diagram. Bring the needle back up at C, then into the fabric vertically above A.

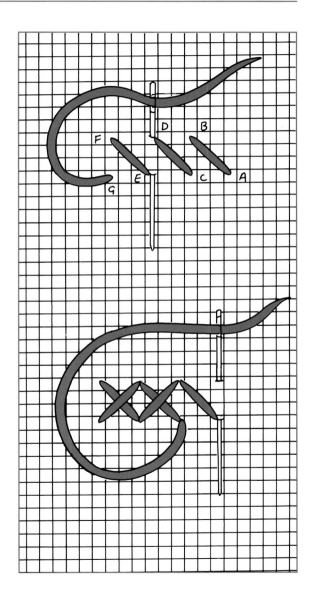

SPACED CROSS STITCH

For some designs the cross stitches are placed with
gaps between them, rather than touching.

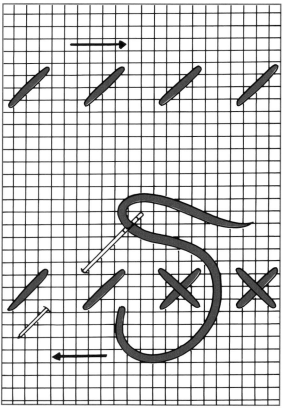

The rows can be worked from left to right or vice
versa. Work a complete row of half crosses across
the fabric spacing them as desired. Complete the
crosses on the return row. This method also forms
spaced cross stitch on the reverse of the fabric.

DOUBLE CROSS STITCH

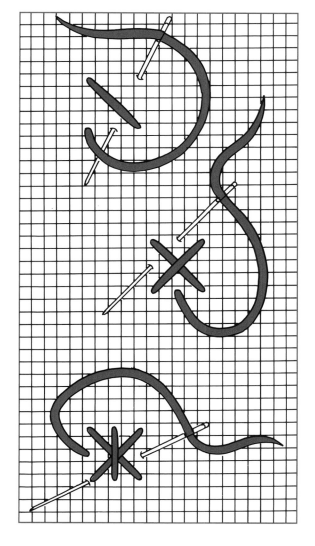

This stitch covers a square of fabric made up of four horizontal and four vertical (or any even number) threads.

1 Work a single cross stitch in the usual way, then bring the needle out of the fabric in the centre of the base of the cross (see page 59).

2 Take a straight vertical stitch over the cross and into the fabric, coming out in the centre of the left-hand side. Take a straight horizontal stitch across the cross to complete the double cross, bringing the needle out at the lower left-hand side, ready to work the next stitch to the left of the first.

DOUBLE-SIDED CROSS STITCH

Use this stitch when you would like the finished article to be reversible. The crosses formed will look the same on both sides of the fabric. You will need to go across the fabric four times to complete the stitches.

1 Begin the first row from left to right and work a half cross stitch in the usual way but on alternate stitches (see page 61).

2 Work back across the row, completing the crosses over the same stitches but making the first diagonal in this row in two halves, as shown in the diagram.

3 Go back across the row again this time working half cross stitches in between the previous cross stitches.

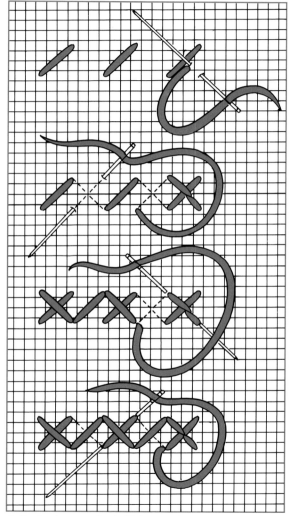

4 Go back over the half diagonal, taking the needle into the fabric in the middle of the righthand cross

and out again at the bottom lefthand corner of this
cross.

5 Finally work back again completing these cross
stitches.

ITALIAN CROSS STITCH
This stitch, a cross set in a square of straight stitches,
is worked in two journeys across the fabric and is
also reversible.

1 Begin in the bottom lefthand corner and work in
horizontal rows. Work the first half cross stitch,
bringing the needle out of the fabric at the base of
the same stitch (see page 63).

2 Work a vertical straight stitch up to the same
level and bring the needle out at the bottom right
hand side, ready to complete the cross on the
wrong side of the fabric.

3 Make a horizontal straight stitch to the corner
and back out of the fabric in the same hole. Then
work the next stitch in the same way and continue
in this way to the end of the row.

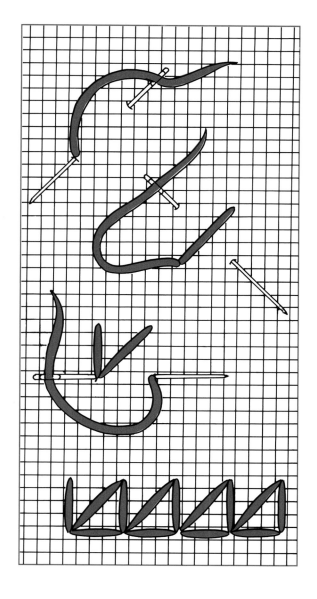

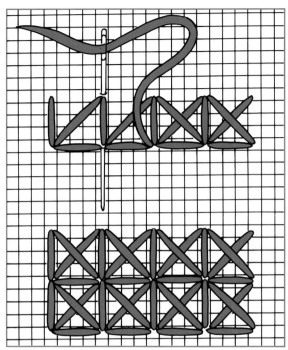

4 To complete the crosses, work back over the row stitching the second diagonal.

5 The second row completes the stitches in the first row. If only one row is required or to complete the final row, after working the second half of each cross, bring the needle out at the top of the first half and work a horizontal stitch across the top.

MONTENEGRIN STITCH

This elongated cross stitch is bordered with straight stitches. Work this stitch in rows from left to right.

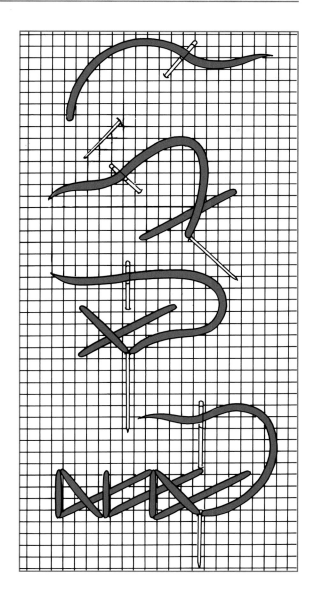

1 Bring the needle out of the fabric and make a diagonal stitch to the right four threads up and eight threads to the right (see page 65). Bring the needle out of the fabric four threads to the right of the base of the first stitch.

2 Make a short diagonal stitch to the left, taking the needle over four threads up and across. Bring out the needle where it last emerged.

3 Make a vertical stitch over four threads and bring out at the same point as before. Repeat to form the next stitch.

LONG-ARMED CROSS STITCH

As its name implies, this is another elongated form of cross stitch. Work this stitch in rows from left to right.

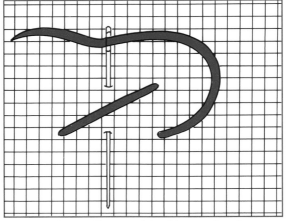

1 Bring the needle out of the fabric and make a

long diagonal stitch four threads up and eight
threads to the right. Bring the needle out four
threads vertically below.

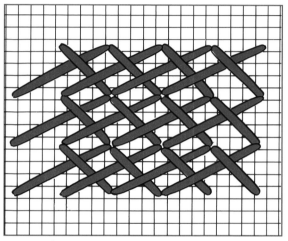

2 Form the cross stitch by taking a diagonal stitch
left four threads up and four threads to the left.
Bring the needle out four threads vertically below,
ready for the next stitch.

RICE STITCH
(WILLIAM AND MARY STITCH)

This stitch covers the background fabric well, adding a raised texture. Work the stitch in two colours for decorative effect.

1 Work a basic cross stitch over four threads (or any even number) over the chosen area (see page 69).

2 Bring the needle out centrally at the top of the stitch. Take a small back stitch diagonally at right angles over two threads and over each arm of the cross, so mini crosses are formed.

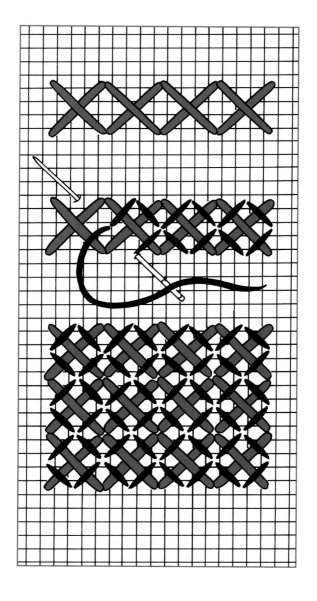

ONE-SIDED INSERTION STITCH

This is a complicated looking cross stitch. It is
worked from right to left across the fabric.

1 Work a diagonal stitch four threads to the right
and four threads up (see page 71). Bring the needle
out of the fabric horizontally, four threads to the left
and take a diagonal stitch to complete the cross.

2 Come out of the fabric horizontally four threads
to the left. Make a diagonal stitch four threads to
the right and eight threads up. Come out of the
fabric horizontally four threads to the left.

3 To complete the irregular cross, insert the needle
in the fabric at the righthand top of the first cross
stitch. Come out of the fabric horizontally eight
threads to the left.

4 Form a second simple cross stitch and come out
of the fabric at the top left of this last cross. Now
insert the needle eight threads down and four
threads to the right. Come out of the fabric
horizontally four threads to the left

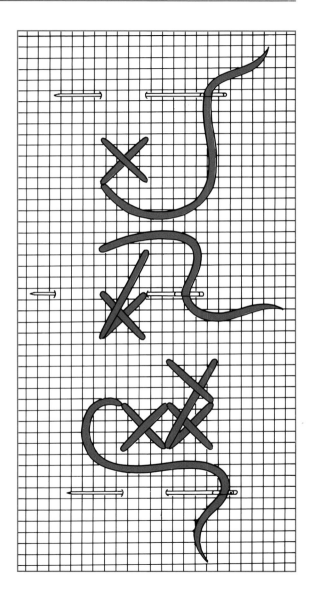

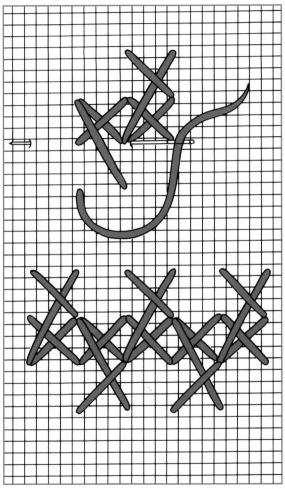

5 Take a diagonal stitch four threads up to the right to complete the irregular cross. Continue in this way. Work the next row either above or below, so that it fills in the spaces left in the first row.

TWO-SIDED INSERTION STITCH

This is also a fairly complex stitch forming triangles of crossed threads.

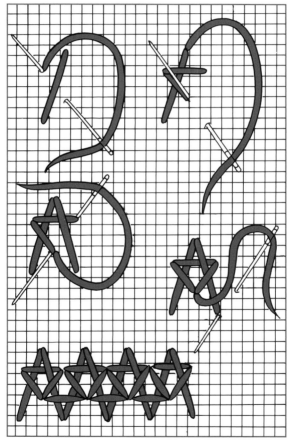

1 Take a diagonal stitch two threads to the right and seven threads up. Come out of the fabric two threads down and two threads to the left.

2 Take a diagonal stitch three threads down and two threads to the right, coming out at the beginning of the same stitch.

3 Take a horizontal stitch to the right over four threads, coming out at the top of the first long diagonal stitch.

4 Insert the needle again four threads to the right of the base of the first stitch and come up two threads up and two threads to the left.

5 Make a diagonal stitch two threads to the right and three threads up, coming out at the beginning of the same stitch.

6 Take a horizontal stitch to the right over four threads, coming out at the base of the second long diagonal stitch. Continue in this way.

This stitch forms diamonds on the back of the work as shown below.

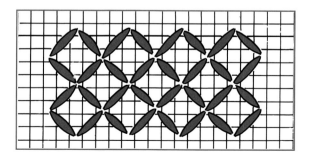

HUNGARIAN CROSS STITCH

These couched cross stitches are worked over a group of laid threads.

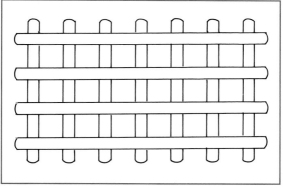

1 Work an evenly-spaced grid of laid threads across the area to be stitched, leaving at least one horizontal and vertical fabric thread between.

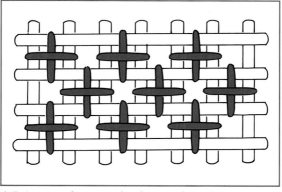

2 Bring out the second colour and work a vertical and then a horizontal stitch over the centre of the laid threads, forming the design.

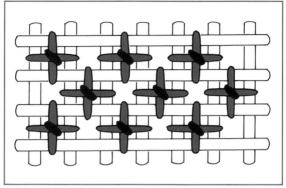

3 Each of the cross stitches is then couched down diagonally across the centre, either using the same colour or working in a contrast.

HERRINGBONE STITCH
A continuous type of cross stitch. It can be worked to different heights and widths. If the stitches in the top and bottom rows touch each other, "Closed herringbone stitch" is formed.

1 Bring the thread through the fabric at A, insert the needle at B, three threads down and three threads to the right of A (see page 77). Bring the needle out at C, three threads to the left of B.

2 Insert the needle at D, six threads up and six threads to the right. Bring the needle out at E, three threads to the left of D.

3 Reinsert the needle at F, six threads down and six threads to the right. Bring the needle out at G, three threads to the left of F.

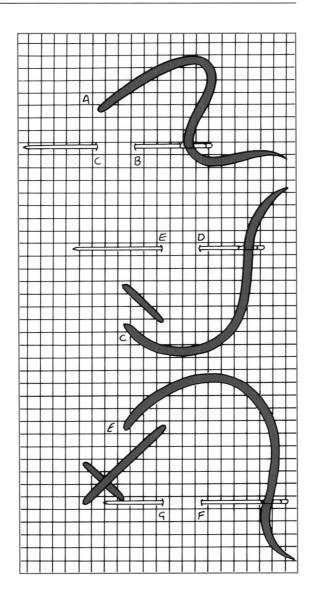

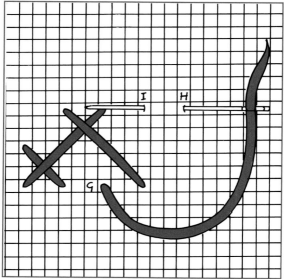

4 Take the needle up to H, six threads up and six threads to the right. Bring the needle out at I, three threads to the left of H. Continue in this way to the end of the row.

DOUBLE ALGERIAN CROSS STITCH (DOUBLE HERRINGBONE STITCH)

This stitch is two rows of interlaced herringbone stitch, worked in contrasting colours. Each row is worked slightly differently from the standard herringbone stitch. Work both rows from left to right.

1 Using the first colour, bring the needle out on the bottom line, insert it diagonally four threads right and four threads up and take a horizontal stitch

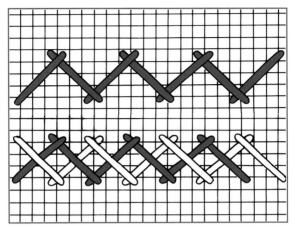

under one thread from right to left along the top line of the row.

2 Slipping the needle under the stitch, make a diagonal stitch four threads down and four to the right and insert the needle on the bottom line, taking a horizontal stitch from right to left under one thread. Continue in this way, always slipping the thread under the diagonal stitches.

3 Use a contrasting thread for the second row. Bring the needle out directly above the first stitch and take a diagonal stitch four threads down and four threads to the right.

4 Take a horizontal stitch under one thread on the bottom line from right to left directly below the first stitch.

5 Take the needle under the diagonal stitch just made and under the diagonal from the first row and make a horizontal stitch in the centre of the next stitch on the top line. Go over the next diagonal stitch and make another horizontal stitch on the base line. Go under the next stitch and continue across the fabric.

GREEK CROSS STITCH

This filling stitch consists of rows of Greek cross stitches. To stitch the lacy filling, work in diagonal lines across the fabric. All the stitches must be firmly pulled. The stitches can also make a square formation. Again pull the stitches to achieve the open effect.

1 Bring the needle through the fabric at A (see page 81). Insert at B, four threads up and four threads to the right. Bring out at C, four threads down, keeping the thread under the needle point.

2 Pull the thread through and reinsert the needle at D, four threads to the right and bring it though again at C, four threads to the left, as shown.

3 Pull the thread through and insert the needle at E, four threads down and bring it through again at C, four threads up, keeping the thread under the needle point.

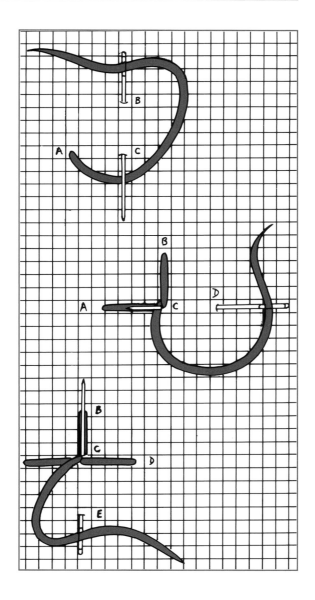

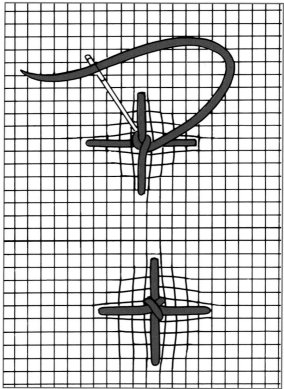

4 Pull the thread through, and to secure the cross, insert the needle again at C, overlapping the last and the first stitches, bringing the needle up again at E to make the next stitch.

MARKING CROSS STITCH
This stitch was often used in olden days to mark linen or work monograms. The diagram on page 85 shows the stitches on the other side of the fabric.

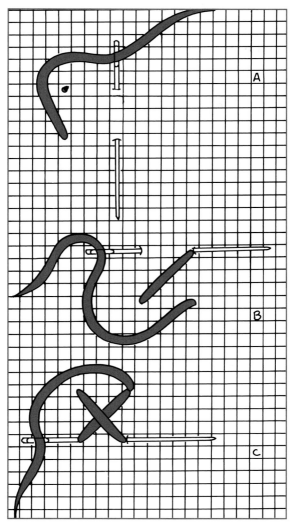

1 Begin at A and work a single cross stitch, as shown in the first three diagrams.

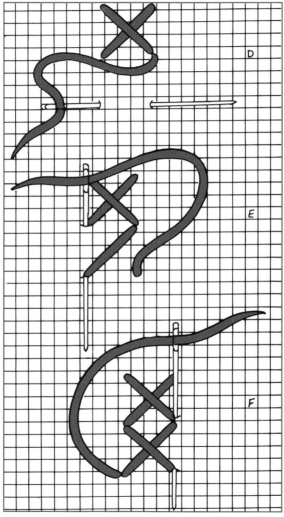

2 The second cross stitch is worked underneath the first. This cross is completed by working over the first diagonal again and the needle returns to the base of the second cross, as shown in the second three diagrams (left).

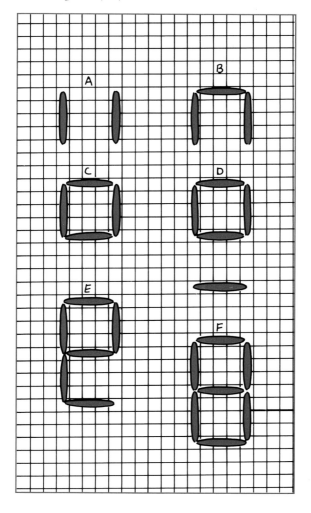

BACK STITCH

Often used as an outline stitch to delineate areas of a cross stitch design or to add extra detail within a particular motif.

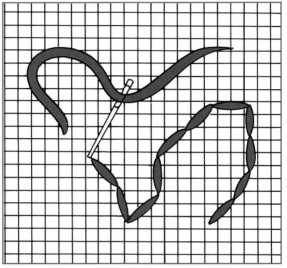

1 Bring the needle out of the fabric. Take a backward stitch, bringing the needle out the same distance in front of the point where the thread emerged.

2 Take the needle back over the space and bring out the same distance in front. Repeat across the fabric as required.

HOLBEIN STITCH (DOUBLE RUNNING STITCH)

Another outlining stitch often used in Assisi work.

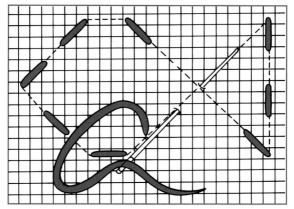

1 Work a basic row of evenly-spaced running stitches along the outline.

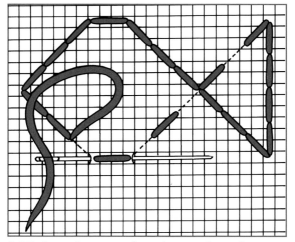

2 Work another row of evenly-spaced running stitches but in the opposite direction, so that the second row of stitches fills in the spaces left in the first row.

RANDOM STITCHING

This is used in free-style embroidery and does not
have to be worked on an evenweave fabric (see
page 29). Work cross stitches of different sizes all
over the fabric, without counting any threads.
Work in groups or individually.

Part 4:
CARE AND DISPLAY

CLEANING

Because of all the handling, you may find that the fabric looks a little grubby after the embroidery is finished . So before the piece is framed or finished, you may need to launder it.

If the embroidery has been worked in colourfast threads on a washable fabric, the piece can be gently washed in cold water with a mild soap powder. Test a sample if you are not sure.

After washing, rinse thoroughly, then lift out of the water. Do not wring. Lay on a clean towel. Roll up the towel, keeping the fabric flat, to remove excess moisture. Leave to dry.

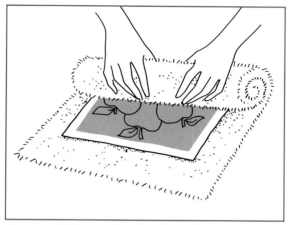

To wash delicate embroidered work, make up a strong mixture of salt and warm water and soak the fabric overnight. Next day, dip in a warm soapy mixture to remove the salt.

If the threads or fabric cannot be washed use a reliable stain remover, having first tested it on a spare piece of fabric. Alternatively, take the embroidery to a dry cleaner.

PRESSING

Before framing or mounting press the embroidery
well.

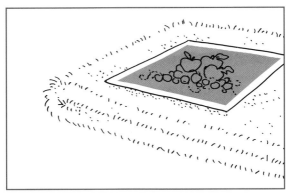

Lay a folded towel over the ironing board. Place the
embroidery face down over the towel.

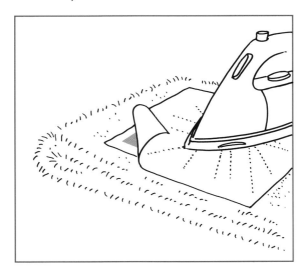

Cover with a damp cloth. Press lightly on the embroidered areas pressing the surrounding fabric in the usual way. If the fabric is damp from washing, cover with a dry cloth and press in the same way.

DISPLAY

Cross stitch can be displayed in a variety of ways from pictures and cards to bell pulls and pendants. Embroidery stores and mail order catalogues display a wide range of pieces just for this purpose. Cross stitch can even be worked on fine fabric and used to cover button moulds for clothes.

Index